T0196952

# NONSENSE
## *Creatures*

BRIAN C. ALEXANDER

authorHOUSE®

*AuthorHouse™*
*1663 Liberty Drive*
*Bloomington, IN 47403*
*www.authorhouse.com*
*Phone: 1 (800) 839-8640*

*Cover Artist Credit: Brian C. Alexander*

*Published by AuthorHouse 12/07/2015*

*ISBN: 978-1-5049-6701-3 (sc)*
*ISBN: 978-1-5049-6700-6 (hc)*
*ISBN: 978-1-5049-6730-3 (e)*

*Library of Congress Control Number: 2015920106*

*This is a work of fiction. All of the characters, names, incidents, organizations, and dialogue in this novel are either the products of the author's imagination or are used fictitiously.*

*Print information available on the last page.*

*Any people depicted in stock imagery provided by Thinkstock are models, and such images are being used for illustrative purposes only. Certain stock imagery © Thinkstock.*

*This book is printed on acid-free paper.*

# Contents

# Introduction

Of the many subjects, genres and structures that can make up a poem or story, one can't help but ponder the infinite number of possibilities able to be expressed through these forms. What follows is a collection of stories and poems, strung together by my efforts to create a personal log of my most cherished works. Though not all the themes of these stories and poems are the same, they nonetheless play off one another like a melody of harmonious dissociation. It is through this disconnection that I label them Nonsense Creatures.

# Isle Del Keep

Catapult me into a dream
Morning skies are not what they seem
Waiting like a fool on the beach
Waiting for the girl of my dreams

In the air, a far display
Sandcastles crafted to clay
The tower light reflecting the sun
Knowing she's the only one

No boats to broaden the shore
No rafts to aid in the course
Stedfast, the waves have gone deep
Gone unto the Isle Del Keep

Strung a sailboat from my heart
Sun goes down, nearer the dock
Almost to that castle, clay
See my love, and that's the way

# Dear Friend

I love you far and deeper than the lowest lovely ocean.
I love you far more higher than the widest blue-eyed sky.
I love you for the person I can be when I'm around you.
I love you, now, for always and I never question why.

# Sphere of Passion

As the positions which draw our breath
Delve us deeper into temptation,
As well, we are the victims of good
Nature's most ancient fruit, and the act
Which we call sin doth purify the
Urge, to urn for this urge no longer.
Call me what thy will, with the foulest
Words thou can muster, but riddle me.
Why these beauties that dance across my
Subconscious should be distant, as the
Love that they harbor lies all too near.

# Mr. Ripper

If liver's for dinner
Let heart be for lunch.

Sophisticated, are you not?
Walking softly, cold, distraught.
Silver dangles from your fingers
Bring the cold of endless winters.

Mist-like wind is stalking souls,
Drenched until you've met your goals.
Tingling arms bring failing hearts.
Take them whole or torn apart.

With your top hat and a cane,
Build upon the work of Kane.
Who you are, we'll never know,
Mr. Ripper, ever-told.

If liver's for diner
Let heart be for lunch.

# Grey Birds Melody

A chirping noise heard all around
Soon disappeared without a sound.
It was the grey birds lovely call.
The avian, to all, stood tall.

It leapt upon the shallow air,
With graces drifting like a hair.
It fell into a rhyming pond.
The urge to sing is what I longed.

The grey bird sung a tune of blue.
Its lightened whistles rang, a-coo.
I called him near, but he did hide,
Into the pines, now lost inside.

I hurried quick, right after him.
The grey-winged bird flew through the dim.
A tree concealed grey's kindly glee,
A melody I'll never see.

Now grey bird sits atop that tree,
Always staring down at me.
Seems so peaceful, seems so pure.
He'll sing again, of this I'm sure.

# How the Griffin Felt

The sky was no relief
To a beast who wore a wreath.

Who never knew to fetch,
And witness to a breath
Is how the griffin felt,
Atop the wooden shelf.
The light became a daze,
Then hope became a maze,
The beating of its wings,
Would signal eager kings.

At night, when called to dine,
It walked a seamless line.
Not any fish as rare,
Would singe it's golden hair.
There never came a time,
It fought to save its shrine.
Common men beheld,
A griffin's shining pelt.

The sky was no relief
To a beast who wore a wreath.

# Sea of Divergence

Amiss the stormy seas of love
I look to all, but not above.
This shipwrecked scourge within my chest
Convinces me of seamless rest.
A shattered jar of bloody rum
Spills to the floor amongst the scum,
A crew of cowards scared to face
The touch of any other race.

It almost seems too faint to feel
The rapid lashings at my heel.
Feet churned raw from running scared,
While doubts and failures singe my head.
Lies so deep that dead men crawl
To break their binding from the wall,
Which holds them close with chains of steel
And dries them clean of feeling real.

And so their souls would shrink and fade
Into the dusk, and swoon the wraith.
The reaper's close, and with no fear,
To take the souls he now holds dear.
So then, the waves would clash and scream
Aside the ship where sirens sing.
Unto their call, my heart would dance,
Unforgiving to their trance.

# Twelve Little Men

Twelve little men, they sat on my shelf,
Kicking the wall
And ringing their bells.

Down, they did fall when I would come home,
Into the floor boards,
They'd leave me alone.

Their voices were nebbish and so were their shoes.
They sung out in harmonies,
Ones and in twos.

I took a bite out of one every night.
They sat there like imps,
Never put up a fight.

They laughed while I slept, they wept when I cried.
They smiled with frowns
On the day that I died.

So, seven men sit on the shelf in my room,
I don't doubt they'll find
A new owner soon.

# Delia

Delia, my darling,
My dancing, devious delight.
Name me the ways you intend to love me.
Glare at the women who strive for my gaze,
Turn loose the men who tread near.
Delia my darling,
Stride in monogamy, riddled with fear.

Delia, my sweet-heart,
My jittery wifey, so true.
Count me the days you intend to love me.
Share in the glory of god's solemn vow,
As we do pass through the years.
Delia, my sweet-heart,
Bring me the axe dear, that time is now near.

# Quote of a Strange Old Man

Sit and listen weary
To my story, old and eerie,
And pray you know me well
When the death-clock tolls it's bell.
I'm the man that passes poetries
To the damn-full, waste-full, orally.
Do pray you own my trust,
When your soul should end in dust.

# Vacant Heart Kingdom

And so with the call of the winter,
And the breeze running far along spring,
My heart could remember no other,
Than the girl whom I though was a queen.

Her appearance was gallant and cheerful,
Her voice, how it forced me to sing,
Now I sit and I wonder and pity,
That girl whom I thought was a queen.

In the terms which transcended my values,
And the risks that cold heated love brings,
I cannot forget dancing with her,
The girl whom I thought was a queen.

Though the dusk and the clouds all move weary,
There's inner pain healing a sting,
Now she's off and her life seems so depthless,
The girl whom I thought was a queen.

# Fear's Face

Tis' I who wears the mask,
The mask that swallows souls.
I found it in a grave,
A gravestone marked with bones.

The spirits have no fortune,
The souls refuse to rest,
And in this facial structure
Lies a demonic crest.

No treatment in the Earth
Could conjure such a sin
As to this masked-creation,
A secret held by Jinn.

The powers now within,
To shield my skin from light
Are worth the mortal efforts,
To never halt the night.

# Phantoms of Bermuda

As the boat wavered,
Unfamiliar airs lingered.
While the cold chill floated,
With liquor, my stomach was coated.
Just along the wooden edges
Came the hands of vile wenches.
Misty hair, without a care,
Hid the deadliest of stares.
Then, the apparitions boarded,
Tobias, too scared, had warded.

As I fell sickly,
Falling deep into the sea,
While my daft spirit wept,
Surface tides began to resurrect.
Reaching up, the damned light found me.
Looking down, watching my body,
A head of heat followed next,
And a kind of dizzy-hex.
Then, my spirit, upward, lifted,
Tobias, beside me, drifted.

# Window Pain

I always though the colorful windows of our town's local church looked so beautiful. The priest, Father Mathieson, would always comment on how he'd constructed the windows himself, showing the struggles of Christ and depicting the commandments. He even began to put up windows depicting the images of local missing persons in the area. He believed that this would help guide their souls to safety, wherever they may be, while keeping them in our thoughts and prayers. It was in this light that, Father Mathieson shined as a beacon of hope for all.

One day after a terrible fight with my husband, I sought refuge and guidance in the house of God. It was Wednesday, and as everyone knows, the church is always briefly closed every other Wednesday. I could not wait and stormed in, asking for forgiveness as I wiped the tears from my eyes and performed the sign of the cross before entering. As I came into the church I took note of the emptiness and startlingly arid atmosphere. I called out for father Mathieson, but he did not reply.

My curiosity got the better of me as I made my way to Mathieson's living quarters. As I entered the farthest room of the chapel I noticed a chalice of red wine sitting on a dark wooden table, which bared the sign of a pentagram. The longer I stared at the red liquid the more I began to realize that it wasn't wine at all. I stepped backwards and swiftly felt a presence behind me. I turned to see Father Mathieson, with widened black eyes and a twisted grin taking up his face. There was blood seeping from his mouth.

There was no place for me to run as I dropped to my knees, begging him for forgiveness, having intruded in his quarters. He put his hand on my head and spoke in a clam voice, his grin never fading. He said I was forgiven and that this "ritual" of his was a personal imperfection which he'd been attempting to cleanse himself of. He told me he harbored no ill-will towards me. Yet, if word of his "ritual" were to get out, he would be pulled from his position as a priest and asked if I would want that, rhetorically.

Before I could reply he stood me up and with a wave of his hand I felt a cool transcendent rush all over me. He told me I would no longer have any worries, as I was forever allowed to dwell in the peace and tranquility of the house of God. I must say, I've never been more at peace. Every Sunday I see my friends' and neighbors' hopeful, smiling faces as Father Mathieson gives a tremendous mass.

I only wish I could talk to them just one more time. I must say, I look so beautiful since Father Mathieson made a place for me to the right the church doors. I only hope the local children don't accidentally throw stones at any of the church windows. Father Mathieson say's we shatter easily.

# The Experimental Cat

I saw that cat pass by my window again. The same cat that was run over by the black prestigious carriage the other day, and the same cat which fell from the third story balcony, miraculously appearing along the sidewalk completely unscathed. The locals joke of the nine lives a cat carries, but never before have I witnessed such prestidigitation on a scale as minimal as this. I take a pen to the flimsy pages of my journal almost every other full moon in hopes of catching each instance of this feline's seemingly final demises. I find no pattern in his deaths, and can draw no conclusion as to why the beast has survived more than twenty four accidents which should have silenced it, permanently.

In some cases it was crushed, burned, and I'm sure even starved at one point, if such an incredible specimen can go without the need for food. I've never heard it speak, but it caries a voice far deeper than the sound of thunder, and I can tell it is powerful. The eyes have seen conflict too great to imagine, and still it's fur, silk and black, can remain dry even after the the most drenching downpours. This cat is almost untouched by life, whilst never harboring the shadow of death. It is caught in-between the two somehow, in a place outside of understanding. I doubt sometimes if it even knows of it's own abilities. If such power did lay within the belly of an animal, why not such power lay within the palm of a man? What could tie a mere cat to the unexplained glitches of the universe, and if studied, could we comprehend it? Could I comprehend it!? Living alone for some time, I had always found comfort in the assurance that any discovery that I couldn't prove to a sceptic party, I could take peace in the belief of knowing myself. I have kept this knowledge about the cat's existence a secret, and I have no intension of telling anyone, for now.

There was a time I had planned and succeeded in experimenting on the beast. I caught it in an alley and lured it with fish. I was stunned to witness that it wasn't devoid of animalistic instinct. For a while I kept it in my two-room home and ran my tests without direction. I found maintaining it's presence in a cage to be the biggest chore, as it would disappear and reappear at random, often walking through walls and laying or walking across vertical or upside-down surfaces. Once I invited the feline into my home, it wouldn't leave, and soon enough, neither could I. It was startling at first, to open my front door or to stare out a window at a world that stretched on for infinite miles, but shrunk to a flat solid picture when it was reached out for. I could only ever leave my apartment when the cat was by my side. Having him around made my mind venture off and contemplate wicked thoughts of more brutal experimentation.

I used stun it with darts. When it was passed out, I'd break it's paws. when it finally came around again it would leap up at me and scratch my face. It would then jump up and begin to walk away, on all fours. A few times I took a knife to it. In one instance I dipped it in a cauldron of acid. Each time the beast came back and treated me with a new scar. It was too amazing to witness. I had to continue my tests! I could feel the cat growing annoyed at my antics, but it wouldn't leave. I fed it, and it did not know that it's hunger was merely an illusion. The beast could not die from starvation, and it clung to me to fulfill this one need. As long as this fact remained a secret I knew it would never leave me. No matter what I put it through. Still, the urge to tests the felines limits and powers wouldn't cease for a long while. It's torture continued to the full enjoyment of my curiosity, and after awhile, hurting this 'god' became fun.

When I would ponder these thoughts I honestly believed he could comprehend what I was thinking. He would follow along with angry looks and hissings that reared from a cat and rung like a cobra. He gave off the presence of so many other animals and displayed that he could even morph himself to appear as them. The beast would spawn in different parts of my apartment, making it quite hard to proceed with testing. I tended to notice that when laying on it's back, spilt liquids in the apartment dripped upwards, then down again when the cat turned over. Alone in my apartment with that entity in the form of a cat was indeed a mind expanding experience. I could almost feel the nothingness in the space outside my rooms. I was in a pocket, cut off from time, with a lazy, presumptuous animal to serve as my only key to the world beyond this place, where dimensions lie scattered and twisted. Then the day came that I would finally execute my final test. This act which I would soon take great regret in knocked at my chest and danced on my mind. I kept my thoughts a blank as I walked over to the beast sitting gingerly at the foot of my bed. I picked it up and pet it's head as I had done time and time again.

With the beast in my hands I made my way over to a desk where I reached for my letter opener, out of the beast's view. I could no longer contain my excitement. The cats face jolted a surprised look at me as his eyes shot wide, keen to my sudden thought. I was quicker then it, and I drove the letter opener into the beast's neck and hacked across with a vicious thrust, ripping and tearing its vocal chords. It screamed out, like a person would and with the sound of a hundred animals, the deeper I cut, the more gargled the scream became before it stopped sounding like an animals. I was covered in blood and my hands shot up to catch air as the beasts body fell from my arms and hit the ground with a vicious thud. My breaths were heavy and I blinked with frantic quickness. By my third blink the cat no longer laid bleeding out upon my carpet. Instead it was perched upon the end of my bed, just as it was seconds before. It glared with a hard discomfort before leaping from my bed and onto the floor. I couldn't tell if I had really just cut the feline's throat, or if I had just imagined the last few seconds.

As I looked down at my arms, the letter opener and my scarlet-soaking arms made it clear, that what I had just done really happened. Once again, within moments of death, the cat miraculously spawned, unscathed, only a few feet from me. Assured, I could do it no harm if I tried… at least, no permanent harm. As as my key to the world outside strolled across the floor, I couldn't blame the beast for what it did next. Across the blood soaked carpet it trailed, and growing transparent with every step. It walked through the door with ease and disgust traveling on its shadow. And suddenly it's presence was gone, and the omnipotent cat had rendered me silent to the world, trapped inside my two-room apartment, with no key to return to the world outside these inescapable dimensions.

I tried stepping outside, escaping through the window, even smashing through the foundation of the rooms to reach the apartments above and below, but there is nothing there. Nothing but condensed space and oblivion. I met a true product of unbelievable scientific existence. It's clear I won't be returning to the reality I'm familiar with anytime soon. I also fail to believe the cat will cross my plain again, after what I'd done to it. I still wonder though, what would it have been like if instead of a beast containing such a gift, the possibilities of a man being created and harboring such abilities? That is the phenomenon I believe mankind will see one day. The difference everyone needs to see to understand our irrelevant roll in this vastly incomprehensible existence. It's the difference that sets men apart from gods, and gods apart from beasts. That is the difference in power.

# Falsified

And what is the use, I implore you?
Now, what is the use, understand!

I haven't the time for a pure-view!
Too busy to try my own hand!

Why bother with what you are spouting?
How dare you expect me to know!

Opinions are weak, you are drowning!
In your pool of words, do please go!

Where now can I find the real answers?
I'd stay far from your bleak line-of-sight!

The molded, to you they are dancers!
A teacher, like you, is not right!

You talk like a snake, one's own charmer!
With those venomous things that you say!

Beware as the molded grow calmer!
Like burnt ashes, we'll blow you away!

# The Dawnstalkers

The Dawnstalkers were everywhere,
In the towns near the Hudson, South.
The village-folk go missing there,
By the time all the crows come out.
They say they dress in black to hid
A pure-white face of all evil.
We try our best to just abide
By our town's evening curfew.
A bridge into town be their way
To cross over to our own plain.
All the old villagers do say,
They'll enter the town if they please.
The full-moon was risen and blue
As the Dawnstalkers came to be.
Townspeople were awed, what to do?
The evil then strode in a line.
It turned us to sin in a day,
And pitied our weak mortal ways.
The lot of us started to fade,
The white-death had made it's cascade.
The blessings hung on the doors
Did nothing to silence this curse.
At mid-day we take to the Mores,
Joining the Dawnstalker's parade.

# 2062

In twenty sixty-two,
The blue day shined a-new,
As humankind would come
To know where they came from.
A lightened day it was,
While 'they' came from above
And landed in the grass,
Attracting echoed-mass.
Their eyes were worth a grasp,
The head could choke a gasp,
And from their ship, they fell
Unto our blue-green Hell.
They left with little haste,
Leaving us with distaste.
The visitors had gone
Without righting the wrong.

# The Problem

What's wrong with you, She asked.
It can't be true, She gasped.
Perhaps It's you, I sassed.
Remove the knife, I tasked.
I can't go on, She passed.
With such good fun, I masked.

# A Wayward

Deeper into the Ether,
Where the sky-sailor sailed, no longer.

Far into the vast,
Till the emptiness did pass.

Beyond the cauldron's handles,
Lies a brew, with tears from the vandals.

Past the rays which preach,
Down the path that does not speak.

# The Radicals

Political squabbles aside,
The surf is bodacious tonight.
The King hath now cast us to death,
We'll drink at the party, till deaf.
Plant bombs in the room with the throne,
My board was hand-crafted at home.
Pour gunpowder down on their wigs,
Quite bogus, these law-uphold pigs!
The revolution, still denied,
With love and peace, do abide.
The victory has shown light,
And corporate has remained uptight.

# The Origin

Poor young James is seldom dead,
With an axe caught in his head.
Further proof of Keith's betrayal,
Organs resting in a pale.

"Nothing to go on" say the cops,
Inspecting flattened Mary Pops.
Her face was rosy, her blood, red rare
Until she'd been found slashed in a chair.

Looks like Keith, the copper played,
While James awoke with a heart and spade.
Eyes so deep the blackness filled,
All the calmness and the still.

Kind Keith Summerholt smothered poor James.
Kind Keith Summerholt got called names.
Kind Keith Summerholt fried like toast.
Killer Keith Summerholt's now a ghost.

On the other side of town
Keith was rising out-of-ground.
James stalked by with butcher knives,
Keith was hit, cried out in lies.

The undead men who fought again,
Slashing innocence with their sin.
Defiled men of life's sick acts,
Smoking gun and a battered axe.

Keith reached into James' chest,
Grabbed his heart beneath his breast.
Tore it out for him to see,
James would then fall on one knee.

Kind Keith Summerholt smothered poor James.
Kind Keith Summerholt got called names.
Kind Keith Summerholt fried like toast.
Killer Keith Summerholt's now a ghost.

Looking at his killer twice,
James did curse this menace lice.
Until life you will stay dead,
Until death you'll live instead.

A paradox of fiendish sorts,
Contorting Keith's malicious torts.
He screamed in horror so sweet to taste,
As muscles tightened like holy lace.

With a crumble James had diminished.
At last Keith's first victim was finished.
Keith, with the red axe, walked down on the street
With the sun rising and blood at his feet.

# Beyond the Aquatic Ether

The dream's imaginary.
The rain falls in your way.
The goals seem too uncanny,
To reach a lighter day.
This shallow boat's unspoken
To the sea that pushes on,
And the waves of understanding
Are what we sail upon.
Break the mighty tide-line,
Increase the will and gloat.
At that night which burns into morning,
And while the past explodes.
All the elements of power
Try their best to hold us near,
And the light of day is a shower
To drown us all in fear.
But the mighty seams of homeland
Put the horror in it's place,
And we wipe the cold shore free of
All the emptiness and space.
To the final destination,
Carry all those who've not fell,
As the mad abomination
Makes the wind to guide our sail.

# Good & Evil (English)

God was a bird
Satan was a snake
God was everlasting
Satan was filled with much hate

God had much grace
Satan was disgraced
God was the eternal
Satan, beneath the Earth, reined

# Bonum & Malum (Latin)

Deus avis
Satan coluber
Deus vitam aeternam
Satan repleta multum odium

Deus gratiam
Satan classes dedecus
Dei aeterni
Satanam sub terra reprimendus

# An Ancient Depth

Let that which does sleep maintain stasis,
As all that have come unto bask.
Encrypted, the knowledge holds weary
To blatant souls brought to the task.

Due, gods with the minds of the gothic,
The winds catch their breath on the mast.
Depths farther than seas running scarlet,
And to these depths, death they do cast.

Fall faint to the call of the elders,
Stand ready to hear their proud heed.
A consciousness swallowed and battered,
The only, the ghastly, the seed.

Cold flesh upon wood in a box-form
Sent burning and into the sea.
As spirits float high to the skies end,
The spirit that stayed here was me.

# Poems By Colleen Debra McCarthy

# Last Breath

Courageously bleeding as she pressed on the blade,
Cowardly disappointed for the mistake she had made.
Disappointed on her spiteful choice,
It wasn't her… It was that unspoken voice.
It took control, she had been mesmerized by the blood,
Dominating her mind like a dreadful flood.
Splitting open her cherry red vein,
Numbed and restrained, feeling no pain.
Shut her eyes, and gasped a last breath,
Awaiting for a dear and peaceful death.
Her wrists began to pour,
Drip dropping like rain, it sprinkled the floor.
Her body became lifeless…
She passed… God bless…

# Cut my Soul in Half

I observe my previous tries,
My unseen hurt and earlier cries.
I couldn't hold back,
As I slice the word fat.
Blood oozes and drips down the drain,
A slight tingle, but no real pain.
It begins to feel so real,
My heart and wounds will never heal.
The more I seem to struggle the chains begin to bind,
It's so disappointing that my happiness, I may never find.

# Blank

Blood poured from my wrist,
Streaming down as I pulse my fist.
Swallowed the pain and tore the skin,
Used my old blood stained pin.
Black blood poured to the floor,
Cry and screaming, slashing for more.
My blood begins to thin, as my vision starts to spin…
"I guess I should have stopped",
..As my limp body dropped..
Cut my Soul in Half

I observe my previous tries,
My unseen hurt and earlier cries.
I couldn't hold back,
As I slice the word fat.
Blood oozes and drips down the drain,
A slight tingle, but no real pain.
It begins to feel so real,
My heart and wounds will never heal.
The more I seem to struggle the chains begin to bind,
It's so disappointing that my happiness, I may never find.

# My Body

You act like your emotions don't matter,
As I sit there and watch your soul shatter.
Slices and slashes lie upon your arm,
Caused by a little thing called self-harm.
Bones protrude from your skin,
My poor body, she's stick thin.
Not only were you as thin as a rail,
Your face was turning deathly pale.
My body was slowly dying,
My insides were torn and I was stuck crying.
You begun to drop buckets of blood,
Seeping through your veins, the floor starts to flood.
Your eyes turned black and tears dripped down,
You drop…
Lifelessly lying on the ground.

# Not So Caught, The Anticlimactic

Of all the many possibilities which can befall a naive young man wandering the streets of a cold Boston town at the stroke of midnight, who would conclude that he would fall victim to a force which lurks farther in the shadows than any strobe of insufficient light would care to venture. While it is in the nature of all malevolent things to be swift and to act to serve a kind of psychological need, this particular event, alongside the gruesome aftermath which was discovered merely seconds before dawn, was a bitter display of a sinful enjoyment, as the murderous scene displayed a depth of fulfillment which must have spanned a fraction of the nightly hours. In the short amount of time it took for the surrounding law enforcement to come to an agreement upon the nature of the following night's murder, as well as the proceeding ones that had all followed closely collaborated characteristics, I was already knocking on the doors of suspects from Roxbury to Allston with a keen suspicion.

In a broad speakeasy I found a man by the name of Robert Kingsly, running one of Charlestown's greatest entertainment establishments, with the help of a few shady figures whom I was unable to identify despite my extensive research and background checking. I could only assume that the men venturing in and out of Mr. Kingsly's establishment all day and night would be the only few individuals, in this area, to walk the desolate streets at night with just cause, but absent of a motive, as well as being able to provide alibis on the night of every murder that'd been taking place those past few months. Resorting to the act of stalking, I followed up on the after-work activities of all of Mr. Kingsly's illegal helpers, going so far as to hold their fear for discovery on the line in an attempt to gain more information, as well as a means of testing their provoke-ability.

Even Mr. Kingsly checked out, in his foot suit, obsession for cigars and love for never finishing a full word. He was cleared of my suspicious which in turn landed me a position on his bad side, shocked that an ammeter detective of my nature would suspect such a largely established man of his stature. He was fat-headed, and so was I after I was knocked out, cold and dead with a pipe the following night.

What a shame it was too. I'm not sure what it was I missed in Mr. Kingsly's establishment. I didn't get a glance at the man who killed me, hell, I can't even remember what had brought me there that night.

All I know is that this case is over for me before it even began, and that's the shittiest part. That is, aside rom walking the Earth in limbo. Death is a bitch, but then again, so is life.

# The Mind Plant

I was particularly unaware of when my uncle, Professor Thomas Arthur Lyncroft, first made contact with the bizarre plant that sat within a cardboard box, wrapped in brown paper and tied with string, atop the highest shelf of his dust-ridden study. As his most curious and convincible nephew, it didn't take long for me to respond to my uncle's invitation. An invitation to stay with him for a month or so in his dubious Boston estate, a cornfield away from the prestigious Sutwell University where he taught biology and every that cursed creationism. In this month or so he would teach me the basics of what a biologist would have to prepare for, if I would ever plan to one day find myself before students of my very own, handing down the teachings of my uncle and late father, and making a name for myself, following the Lyncroft legacy.

My uncle was going to teach me so much. I am now startled to say that over time a kind of dark-influence fell over my uncle, leading to his untimely death, and at my hands. While I struggle to tell myself that it was out of mercy, part of me couldn't help but muster a hatred for my uncle, and for this thing he so ignorantly flaunted as his greatest find. Pulling back the clock to my arrival in Boston, my uncle wasted no time in showing me to the chambers where had stowed the thing away. Much of his behavior had struck me as peculiar, when I first saw him, such as his appearance and mental state. He was a skinny man who looked like he'd never slept. His speech was staggering and his moments were shaky. He looked uneasy with every moment that passed him by, and with this strangeness about him, I kept my distance.

When I was brought to his lab, the plant was displayed on table before me. Bits were glowing as the yellow and hot pink spotted pedals flowed out, down to the dark stem and thorn-spiked leaves. The only odd thing about the plant, that struck me at least, was crystal-like quills that glowed with a dark purple which grew out from the base of the plant. My uncle would not reveal to me about where he had gotten the thing, and would rather avoid the question, change the subject or dismiss my question with another question. I quickly ceased asking and merely shared in his investigation of the plants' genetic make-up. My first week in his estate was spent alongside him, examine the specimen. It wasn't too long before I began to notice the plant seemed to have a defense mechanism. When the thing was met with an object that could slice or press through any surface of it, the purple quills, at the base of the flower, would fire-out like those of a porcupine.

It would take twenty-four hours for the plant to grow back new quills, and every attempt to dissect it would be met with this resistance. I didn't think to ask the major questions during the start of the examinations, as my uncle seemed defensive about delving into the origins of the flower. This led me to finally ask about a bizarre series of green vessel-like tubes which had embedded themselves on my uncles arm, and all of a sudden. This was something he could not hid, as with each day the hole from which the vessels came would glow with a brighter shade of purple. He gave way rather quickly, as he explained a mishap that occurred during his first examination of the planet. He admitted to being hit with one of the quills and suffering a mild decrease in energy as well as a multitude of physical abnormalities. My uncle assured me that the effects of the quills "toxins", as he called them, were merely temporary and that he was feeling fine.

I did begin to notice a great difference in his appearance. He looked healthier, happier and more energetic. I believed all was well, until a midnight stroll through the estate brought me peering through a keyhole of his study, lured by whispers and the sounds of conflicted ramblings coming from my distraught uncle. I had heard him from the hallway and couldn't believe the panic he was in. The plant sat on his desk, still and glimmering. The brighter the quills shined, the brighter his vessels on his arm lit up, and the more historical he became. I began to realize how the mailman and the servants had all ceased coming up to the estate. The gardeners and the groundskeepers hadn't come since I'd arrived either. I noticed that this entire time, the only person I'd seen all month was my uncle, fluctuating in wellness. Deep in thought, I fell forward, slamming open the door and startling my uncle. He looked at me with a vicious glow, grabbing a letter opener, he lunged at me.

I pressed up against the wall and kicked him away into a corner. He was disoriented for a moment as I swiped the letter opener out of his hand and took it to the plant. The purple quills fired, one catching me in my arm. As I pulled it out my uncle jumped on me from behind. As I got myself loose he screamed for me as I ran out the door of the study. He had finally lost it. By the time I had made it to the door he caught up with me, taking time to do something in the study. I ran to the basement where I figured I could hid. Tripping down the wooden steps, and landing at the bottom, I peered through the darkness to see the mangled bodies of the mailmen, groundskeepers, gardeners and household servants, all littered around the cellar. With a sprained arm I stumbled through the pool of blood that made up the basement floor.

Hearing my uncle call out for me once more, I located an axe and took to an area behind the boiler to hide. I believed I was safe, hearing his heated breath come down the basement steps and stepping through the bodies on the ground. He monologged as he searched for me, explaining how ever since he'd been hit with the quill, he began to hear voices. He believed it was the plant, speaking to him, controlling his health and his will, bending his state of mind and informing him of the horrors entailed if he chose to disobey it. He told of how the quills allowed the flower to get into your head, infect you slowly, until your will belonged to it. It was the ultimate defense mechanism, or as I saw it, the ultimate offensive-mechanism. I began to realize that it was no longer my uncle talking. Only the will of the plant exhibited now. My uncle's honesty faded in and out until only the speech of a psychotic hypnotized man remained.

It had taken over my uncle and murdered anyone who wouldn't convert. I hushed my breathing as I waited for the right moment to make for the stairs. This moment came too late as I felt the letter opener from before pierce my chest four times before I fell to the ground. As I looked up, on my back, my uncle stood with wide eyes, bleeding a yellow substance, he grinned and readied the letter opener again. I mustered all my fury and kicked him backward, my chest burning as blood streamed out. My breathing was staggering as I took the axe to my uncle who sat, looking upward at me with saddened eyes, screaming for help as I jammed the axe into his skull again and again. I was screaming with each thrust down, watching his hand reach out for me, I cried when he'd finally stopped moving, and I was sure he was dead. I sat there a long while until my tears dried. I eventually got a hold of myself and made my way back to his study, with a busted arm and four holes on the right side of my chest. So, now that brings us back to the present.

As I sit here, wondering what to do with the plant he packaged up so tightly before coming after me. Part of me would love to tear this damned thing apart, but that'd be too easy. Luckily I haven't forgotten, I pulled one of those quills out of my arm a little while ago. My life and the safety of those around me is compromised. The voices are beginning to set in. There are more than one. That means there must be more than one plant. I feel a collective of sorts, in my brain, intruding and trying to take over. The influence of this hellish flower has taken so many lives, but this one ends with me. I guess I'll just set fire to this whole damn estate. Who'd believe me, secluded in a house full of butchered up bodies. So, I'll burn it all. Thus ends the family legacy of Professor Thomas Arthur Lyncroft and his curious, convincible nephew.

# The Night Shifter

Still, the night offers a presence.
One that brings me forgetfulness.

I report to the world around,
About the lives put in the ground.

From the dusk's arisen shadow
Comes a specter, foul and narrow.

An amazing feat has happened.
These streets are no longer blackened.

For the man who could change his shape
Has fallen to my trap and bait.

No one believes me, and I know
I guess that's how this story goes.

Cast away from the ears of those
Who once heard my honest-true woes.

Will a need for action arrive
Once again, while I am alive?

# The Estate of Victor West

The estate of Victor West
Was mundane at best.
Creepy halls with shadow-men
Nullified the den.

The Foyer, so dark.
The Kitchen, well carved.
The Attic, quite stark.
The Closets, un-barred.

The Bedrooms, well lit.
The Study, too full.
The Basement, true grit.
The Graveyard, as full.

Carpets stained with scarlet-blood,
From the grave came mud.
Swords hung high upon the wall
Fell to halt the waltz.

# Colleen

On a lake not too far from a brook,
Near a river not far from a stream,
I walked with a snow-white lit beauty.
An angel who's name was Colleen.
Amidst all our talk and discussion
Here eyes, and how they drifted so lean,
Hair black as the nightly sky whistled
And whistled to signal Colleen.
A smoke filled the morning she woke to,
Her heart waking up quick with a gleam
It was unto me whom she spoke to.
A speaking and kindred Colleen.
A meal in the evening brought laughter,
An apatite breaking at the seam,
Fulfilled was the hearty meals' balance
To humble and famished Colleen
So meek in the garden with Tootsie,
The chickens and puppies all too keen.
There sat the young girl with her kindness.
A girl by the name of Colleen.
Now say what you will to your mistress.
Insult your partner in a daft scene.
But never speak down on my muses,
Each one of them, only Colleen.

# The Shadows of Eve

The sun turned a brightened blood color,
The sky started turning dim black,
The only sounds heard were thin whispers,
The Shadows of Eve had arrived.

All men who saw unfit to freedom,
All men who could hide who they were,
All men who think greed is not plenty,
Be warned by the Shadows of Eve.

The Shadows turn flowers to dust-hills.
The Shadows, they do not forgive.
The Shadows, they've come for the vengeful,
And reap on the dim Night of Eve.

All those who think they should be weary,
All those with a soul made of coal,
All men who think good is uncanny,
The Shadows will now take your soul.

So here ends the Night of the Shadows,
The Night of the Shadows of Eve.
Till next year, the wicked be worried,
The Shadows shall come while you sleep.

# Cats & Crows

Calling high to the shadows in the sky,
Come down upon my wrist.
To look upon your glide
Is to see death, and die.
See that I wake each day.

Calling low to the shadows on the ground,
Come up-upon my step.
Wait outside the door, meek,
A day, a month, a week.
See that I seize the day.

Calling high to the harbingers that fly,
Brush near so I may note.
Carry words on thy foot,
With a string to assure.
See that I make it through.

Calling low to the specter on the street,
Brush by with your black-coat.
Be my karma, the worst,
Set aside, in my hearse.
See that I leave tonight.

# Gilgamesh IX

The king who was dethroned by a man of
Much hair, was also the man in search of
His ancestor, who knew eternal life.

Through the mountains were tree-gods were supreme,
Past the clouded fields of a dream-like realm,
Upon the tallest peak of Earth, he sat.

An Epic forged by those with redemption
Did little to lessen the fear of death.
Granted by the gods, eternal life hid.

The story of the wandering king is
One that gives little to the essence of
Righteousness, and grants a preservation.

# The Funny Servant

Now we will join the jester
In the chamber down the hall.

Behind the suit and make-up
Sits the butler, standing tall.

He serves the earl in the day
And dances to themes at night.

The servant strides to act right.
Called away, he's out of sight.

Consoling his lord in dusk,
Belittling him in day.

Even on holiday, the man
Who serves will not go away.

When the man of the house does
Pass away, the servant stays.

To aid in the growth of the
Family, these are the ways.

# How, What, Where and Why

How many worlds can there be?
How many lives can we live?
How many times may we love?
How many are there like me?

What is a life worth?
What is a concept?
What is perception?
What are the reasons?

Where does all our time go?
Where can our time be saved?
Where do we both end up?
Where can we find the true start?

Why can't we just say what we mean?
Why must we always make it hard?
Why can't we go back to the start?
Why are we here, and is this real?

# End to a Journey

To sum up the completion of such a task,
I ask you bid me farewell upon my grasp.

I've walked the many miles to make it here,
Enduring contemplation of my past years.

So long to the few who've guided me this far,
Our memories are stuck, molded in a tar.

Quiet now is the wind which kept us from here,
This place where air has gone silent to the ear.

I play upon my flute, and melodies sing,
Recalling all the virtues of which we've seen.

In the field of pedals and grass grown to stay,
Close your eyes and ponder that which made this day.

# The Low Goal of Professor Hagon

I read aloud the passage as my staggering nephew sat in front of me, grasping the arms of his study's desk-chair and sweating with agony. Though the rhyme had no relevance, it seemed poetic at the time to read to him a short collaboration of nonsensical, yet darkly themed, thoughts from a reasonable enough passage. Highlighting the philosophical nature of this occasion, I made my way over to the seat where he lied dying, and looked upon him as a poor animal being put down.

I told him of the circumstances that lead to his imminent demise, as he glared up at me with eyes crafted from all the dying fury he could muster. I could feel the hate emanating in heat and unable to escape through any simple action. For him to even stand now would be a miracle. The seconds would pass away as his heart faded with unending moments, that was, until finally his heart would stop. A drop of custom-poison in his tea would halt any further attempts to secure my estate.

Being a man of much valor, my reputation as a feared professor and positions of power would all be removed from beneath me, had this fool opened his mouth to the authorities. Too many bodies have been buried under me to jeopardize the construction of my empire and any future plans. If I were to die, then it must be known full and well that I accomplished this one task. That task being the completion of my home and complete control over this land and the family fortune. This temple, for which my already damned soul would be free, to roam with ease for an eternity.

I would be free from the shackles of Hell, unending, and unbound to the kingdom of Heaven, existing in a domain of my own. Limbo, where I could rest in anxiety, but none of this would be possible without the death of a family member. Just one. To think, he'd almost foiled me. True it was he that sent the invitation, beaconing me to his mansion in hopes of a talk, working out deals and coming to agreements. My endeavor called for no such civility.

Any and all threats would have to be dealt with swiftly, and with as much force as the consequences would entitle. And so, into his tea, drops of rat poison and toxic chemicals spilt, securing my dream and cutting down every last one of his attempts to best me. This was his punishment for ever believing he could swindle, frame and double-cross me.

Staring at him as he passes away brings a warm comfort to my heart. This warmth spreads to my throat and suddenly I'm choking for air. Poisoned, good lord! I've been poisoned! That snake nephew of mine, running the same rigged game! I never though he would stoop to my level, always parading as the innocent figure, kind to all and scot-free. The bastard!

As I fall to my knees I cannot help but look up and stay fixed on such a scene of irony. I lay at his feet, drooling and gagged, staring at a lifeless youth beside me. He sits like a king, unafraid of his demise, and I lay like a jester at his feet. I fear the end, and it would appear all my preparations have gone to waste.

Turning over, I can see the ceiling closed and dark, my eyes blackening as the poison works deeper and deeper into my soul. The people I've buried surround my grounded-deathbed and look down at me with disgust and anguish. It is this house that I'm to die in, and remain trapped with the ghosts of those I've taken the lives of. Limbo is a dream now, and purgatory is my fate, and that low goal of mine remains unreached, even in death.

# The End

Printed in the United States
By Bookmasters